Our Place in Space

SCHOOL PUBLISHERS

Orlando   Austin   New York   San Diego   Toronto   London

Visit *The Learning Site!*
www.harcourtschool.com

What a Ride!

Earth is always moving. It travels through space at 170,000 kilometers per hour! You can't feel it, but you are rushing through space every moment.

Earth moves two ways. It makes circles around the sun. This movement is called **revolution**. Each trip around the sun takes about 365 days. A year is the amount of time it takes Earth to travel around the sun.

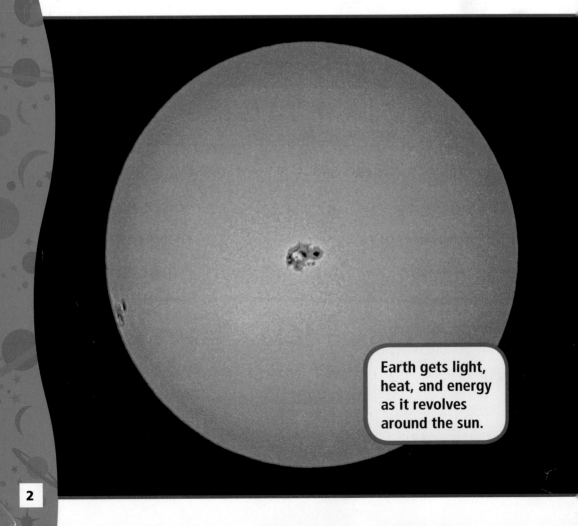

Earth gets light, heat, and energy as it revolves around the sun.

Scientists take photos of Earth from space! This helps us understand Earth's movement.

Earth moves another way. It spins like a top. This movement is called **rotation**. The invisible line that Earth spins around is called its **axis**. The axis goes through the middle of Earth. It goes all the way from the North Pole to the South Pole. Earth is a little tilted on its axis. It takes 24 hours for Earth to complete a rotation. Each rotation is one day.

Earth spins like a top on its axis. At the same time, it travels in large circles around the sun.

MAIN IDEA AND DETAILS **Name two ways that Earth moves.**

3

Passing Time

Here on Earth, day turns to night. Summer turns to winter. How do these changes happen?

You know that Earth makes one rotation every day. It takes 24 hours to complete a rotation. For 12 hours, half of the Earth is facing the sun. It is daytime there. The other half of the Earth is not facing the sun. It is nighttime there. Earth never stops spinning on its axis. Soon, day turns to night and night to day.

When it's daytime in Florida, it's nighttime here in China! As the day starts in China, a person in Florida might be going to bed.

It's a warm and sunny July day in Florida. But it's winter in Australia!

Many places on Earth have four yearly seasons—spring, summer, fall, and winter. The temperature changes each season. It drops in winter. Summer has the highest temperature. What causes these changes?

As Earth revolves around the sun, it tilts on its axis. In the part of Earth that is tilted toward the sun, it is summer. In the part of Earth that is tilted away from the sun, it is winter.

Since Earth stays tilted at the same angle, each place on Earth has the same seasons every year.

 MAIN IDEA AND DETAILS **What makes seasons change on Earth?**

Our Moon

The moon moves, too. Like Earth, it makes revolutions. But the moon doesn't revolve around the sun. It revolves around Earth!

As the moon revolves, its shape seems to change. Some nights, the moon looks round and bright. Other nights, it is shaped like a banana. Some nights, you can't see the moon at all.

The moon does not make its own light. As the moon circles Earth, light from the sun hits different sides of it. The moon reflects the sunlight. From Earth, you see the side of the moon that is lit.

The moon looks as if it changes shapes. Really, you can see only the part of the moon that is lit by the sun. Each shape is a **moon phase**. The moon follows a pattern of phases. This pattern is a **lunar cycle**.

What if sunlight hits the moon from the front? You see the moon in its full phase. It is round and bright. When sunlight hits a side of the moon, you see only that side. When light hits the far side of the moon, you can't see the light—or the moon!

 SEQUENCE Explain how the moon changes phases.

> ### Fast Fact
>
> In 1969, astronauts brought moon rocks back to Earth. Scientists used these rocks to figure out how old the moon was. It's about 4.5 billion years old!

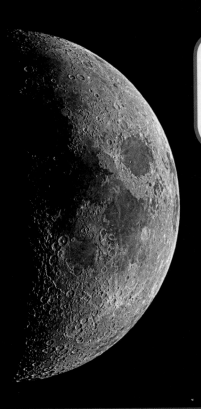

This moon is in its waxing crescent phase. It is on its way to being a full moon.

This moon is in its waning crescent phase. Soon, you won't be able to see the moon at all!

Anybody Out There?

Earth is a planet. A **planet** is a large body of rock or gas in space. The sun is a star. **Stars** are hot balls of glowing gases that give off energy.

The Earth revolves around the sun. The sun gives us energy, heat, and light. There are eight other planets that revolve around the sun. Like Earth, many of these planets have moons. The sun, the planets and their moons, and the small objects that revolve around it make up our **solar system.**

The sun is the center of our solar system. All its planets revolve around it.

The sun gives off so much heat that we can feel it here on Earth.

The sun is not the only star in the universe. There are too many stars to count! You can see many stars at night. All are made of hot gas, but the sun is our closest star. Without the sun, Earth would have no warmth and no light. Some planets in our solar system are much farther from the sun. They are cold and dark. Still, they all get energy from the sun.

 COMPARE AND CONTRAST Compare the sun to other stars in the universe.

Our Neighbors

The four planets that are closest to the sun are known as the inner planets. Earth is one of the inner planets.

Mercury is closest to the sun. It is so hot, that metal would melt on its surface. Mercury is the smallest planet.

Venus is the next planet from the sun. Scientists believe that Venus once had oceans. They are not there anymore.

You can see that Venus does not look like Earth! It no longer has water.

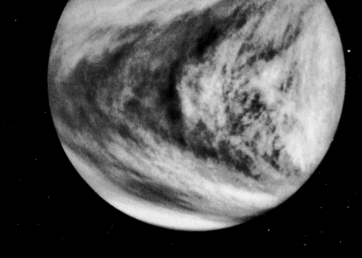

The surface of Mars looks a little like land on Earth. It is mostly rocks.

Earth is the third planet from the sun. It is the only planet that has water on its surface.

Mars comes after Earth. Mars has ice, like Earth. However, most of the ice on Mars is far below its surface.

The inner planets are smaller than the other five planets. Since they are closer to the sun, they are much warmer than the other five planets. They also have rocky surfaces.

 MAIN IDEA AND DETAILS Name the four inner planets.

Spaced Out!

The next five planets are far from the sun. They are much larger than the inner planets. They also are much colder! Many are just balls of frozen gases. The outer planets tend to have many moons.

Mars is the last inner planet. The first outer planet comes right after Mars. It is Jupiter. Jupiter is the largest planet. It has more than 60 moons!

Next comes Saturn. Many people know Saturn because of its rings. They look beautiful through a telescope.

Saturn's rings are made of pieces of ice. Some of the rings are too small to see. Others are wide and bright.

Pluto is the farthest planet from Earth. It's surface is made of frozen gases.

The last three planets are Uranus, Neptune, and Pluto. All three are made from frozen gases. Usually, Pluto is the farthest from the sun. However, it crosses Neptune's path as both planets revolve around the sun. Then, Neptune is the farthest away.

The farther a planet is from the sun, the longer it takes to revolve around the sun. Uranus takes 84 Earth years to make one trip around the sun. Neptune's year lasts about 165 Earth years. Pluto has the longest year. One year on Pluto lasts about 248 Earth years!

Fast Fact

Jupiter has a Great Red Spot that you can see through a telescope. The spot is really a storm—with lightning and great hurricane winds. The storm has lasted over 300 years!

COMPARE AND CONTRAST Compare and contrast the inner planets and the outer planets.

There's More Out There!

Planets, stars, and moons make up most of our solar system. But there are other small objects circling our sun.

Asteroids are like mini-planets that revolve around the sun. Asteroids can fall out of their loop and crash into a planet. A large asteroid could cause big changes on a planet. An asteroid hit Earth near the end of the time of the dinosaurs. Scientists think it changed Earth so much that the dinosaurs died out.

Meteors are small bits of rock and metal. They fall off course and hit Earth. When they do, you see "falling stars."

 CAUSE AND EFFECT What would happen to Earth if a large asteroid crashed into it?

Yearly meteor showers start in July. You can often see these "falling stars" in August.

Fast Fact

Sixteen nations are working together to build the International Space Station. It is being constructed now—in space! When it is finished, astronauts can live there for up to six months!

Space vehicles from Earth have landed on the moon and Mars.

Summary

Earth is hurtling through space! It rotates on its axis as it revolves around the sun. Night changes into day as Earth rotates. As Earth revolves around the sun, our seasons change. During the night, we can see the moon that circles Earth, reflecting sunlight. As our moon goes through its lunar cycle, we see different phases. Earth is one of nine planets that revolve around the sun. Mercury, Venus, Earth, and Mars are the inner planets. Jupiter, Saturn, Uranus, Neptune, and Pluto are the outer planets. These planets, their moons, and the sun are part of our solar system.

15

Glossary

axis (AK•sis) A line you cannot see that goes from the top of the Earth, through the center, to the bottom (3, 4, 5, 15)

lunar cycle (LOON•er cy•kuhl) The pattern of phases of the moon (7, 15)

moon phases (MOON FAYZ•uhz) The different shapes that the moon seems to have in the sky when the moon is observed from Earth (6, 7, 15)

planet (PLAN•it) A large body of rock or gas in space (8, 9, 10, 11, 12, 13, 14, 15)

revolution (rev•uh•LOO•shuhn) The movement of Earth one time around the sun (2, 6)

rotation (roh•TAY•shuhn) The spinning of Earth on its axis (3, 4, 15)

solar system (SOH•ler SIS•tuhm) The sun, the planets and their moons, and the small objects that revolve around the sun (8, 9, 14, 15)

stars (STARZ) Hot balls of glowing gases that give off energy (3, 8, 9, 14)